NURTURE

THE ART OF PARENTING

NURTURE
THE ART OF PARENTING

PETER ALSOP

NATHAN WALLIS

pb potton & burton

DEDICATION

This book is dedicated to all
the parents – past, present,
birth and foster/whāngai – who
have gone above and beyond in
nurturing children's potential.
The social value of that extra
effort – with exponential effect
across activities, relationships
and generations – is immense.

CONTENTS

WELCOME

THANK YOU FOR YOUR INTEREST IN THIS BOOK – WELCOME TO *NURTURE*. IN OUR VIEW, THERE'S NO MORE IMPORTANT HUMAN ENDEAVOUR THAN NURTURING CHILDREN'S POTENTIAL.

We created this book to celebrate great parenting and to share – hopefully in a stimulating way – community wisdom on how to parent even better.

As noted in the book's dedication, the social value of great parenting is immense. While on one level that's obvious, considered more deeply there's the mystery of what *incremental* effect parenting choices have for children over time – the *additional* benefits of good instead of not-so-good choices (or preferably great instead of good). We're also talking about the accumulated social impact, not just for children but on the wider interwoven system as they grow up. This system includes families, teams, organisations, clubs and communities – with impacts year after year after year.

Considered in this light, parenting becomes the cornerstone of community wellbeing and, given such importance, demands careful review. To what extent are children being supported to grow positive emotions? To build authentic connections? To be engaged in absorbing activities when time just disappears? To celebrate a sense of accomplishment? To value a meaningful existence beyond superficial pleasures that quickly pass by?

That formulation of wellbeing is owed to Martin Seligman, the founder of positive psychology and a pre-eminent researcher on human happiness and fulfilment. As discussed in The Story, it's a formula well-worth following and, like all good family recipes, one to use as children develop and then lovingly hand on.

The ingredients also need to be cultivated and grown. On this front, Seligman's research points to developing six human virtues as the fuel of the wellbeing fire. By using the virtues as a structure for this book – wisdom, courage, compassion, integrity, self-mastery and belief – we focus parenting on nurturing the foundations of a great life. In other words, we strengthen the nexus of parenting influence and community wellbeing.

To create this book, we appreciate the gift from a large number of people who trusted us with their parenting ideas. These people challenged the norm – to keep parenting views to ourselves – and embraced what we suggested: It still takes a village to raise great children, and everyday parents have extraordinary ideas that should be shared.

Nurture has been rewarding and enlightening to create. Its real magic, though, will be in the better parenting choices ahead and, through their interwoven and exponential effect, the community of new possibility that awaits. We wish you well for your parenting journey.

THE STORY

THE BOOK STEMS FROM COMMUNITY GENEROSITY AND WISDOM CONTAINED IN 'THE VILLAGE'. IT OFFERS IDEAS TO ENHANCE PARENTING, KNOWING PARENTING IS A CORNERSTONE – IF NOT ULTIMATELY *THE* CORNERSTONE – OF COMMUNITY WELLBEING.

Parenting is intuitive and, in that sense, you'll approach this book bringing your own strengths. We're also not here to tell you what you know. But, as with developing other skills, there's much to be gained from taking a purposeful approach to parenting and learning from each other. Therein lies the book's purpose: to share parenting ideas in the village, in a new, engaging way.

Alongside, we know from experience that many parents are searching for a simple understanding of parenting styles and the impacts of parenting on development of children's brains (the engine room of their growth). As such, parenting ideas – as desirable as they may individually be – should ideally be nestled within a wider understanding of the brain, of parenting styles, and of what we're trying to build: a child's wellbeing.

BUILDING VIRTUES

Like any book, we needed some structure and, for this, turned to the work of Professor Martin Seligman, a professor of psychology at the University of Pennsylvania. Seligman is heralded as the father of positive psychology, a massive contribution to society given the field's focus on building human happiness and wellbeing. Amongst his extensive research, Seligman's key finding for this book is that the development and deployment of six 'humanist ideals of virtue' are pivotal to happiness and wellbeing. This is a finding consistent through time and across cultures – *Mauri Ora*, for example, showed the beautiful alignment of the virtues to the Māori world.[1] For this book, we similarly wanted to show the relevance of virtues to nurturing children and encourage their development from an early age.

So what are these six virtues and what are they fundamentally about? Seligman's work is widely published and well worth a read (his talks on Ted.com or YouTube are also great). For our purposes, we've framed the six virtues in the following simple way:[2]

- **Wisdom** – Cognitive strengths that entail the acquisition and use of all forms of knowledge
- **Courage** – Emotional strengths that underpin the will to take risks and overcome challenge
- **Compassion** – Strengths that involve looking out for and supporting others and ourselves
- **Integrity** – Strengths that underpin strong moral character and support fair and just living
- **Self-mastery** – Strengths that entail understanding, control and tailoring of emotions
- **Belief** – Strengths that forge connections to larger social goals and provide deeper meaning

The virtues are familiar themes. For example, many children will recall a parent or grandparent saying 'don't judge a book by its cover', attempting to avoid judgement and build the virtue of *compassion* instead. In this way, the virtues define our aspirations for the type of people we want to be – and want our children to be.

In short, the virtues *really matter* and as parents we ought to pay attention. But if you're anything like us, when did you last purposefully consider whether you're doing enough to build your child's *wisdom*? Or *courage*? Or scratch beneath the surface of *self-mastery* to consider where your parenting effort might best be placed? By being purposeful, we can unlock our potential as parents to better unlock the potential of our children. We'll come to ideas for doing that, as well as various parenting styles, but what's critical first is an understanding of what we're really trying to nurture: children's brains.

THE BRAIN EXPLAINED

In case you're thinking of skipping the science (which you'd encourage your child not to do!) we need to start quite bluntly: the development of virtues in children, and their ability to deploy them effectively, *directly depends on your own effort* (and the quality of that effort) to develop your child's brain. And does understanding how the brain works enrich our ability to embed virtues into children's lives? It absolutely does.

The brain is complex with many mysteries, but thanks to generations of neuroscientists is now well understood. We know where the virtues are located, how they get there, and how they're built inside the brain. Virtues represent the best of being human, but are *optional* when compared to survival needs such as sustenance and sleep – so this places virtue in the brain's top two layers. As discussed below, these are the parts containing higher intelligence, empathy, self-control and emotional attitudes to life. It is essentially the part of the brain that gives us characteristics of being human; not just an animal focused on mating and survival.

To help understand this, it's useful to think of the brain as a stack of four parts – essentially four mini brains. Just like a tree, a child's brain grows from bottom to top, so brain one is the first to grow and so on (there's some overlap in growth but delineation is useful to explain). And, as you might have guessed, the quality of brain development at the top depends – like any tree – on the quality of growth underneath.

Brain One – Survival

Brain one, the brainstem, governs all the stuff that keeps us alive, such as a beating heart, breathing, and the survival responses of fight, flight or freeze. While as adults we think of compassion or intellect as important, the brain actually sees these as optional – you can live a long time without compassion but not without a beating heart! Brain one, therefore, is initially quite selfish. Only when there's no immediate threat to survival will it allow resources to be handed up to the other brains.

Brain Two – Clockwork

Brain two, the cerebellum, is essentially the clockwork part of being human. As well as movement and motor skills, it performs a regulatory function – knowing when to slow or stop – and plays a foundational role for later development of more advanced cognitive skills. Brain two typically blooms as a baby grows from 6 to 18 months; from a baby happy and content lying down gazing at a parent to an 18-month-old toddler who can crawl, walk, run and use fine-motor skills – all amazingly in a 12-month period.

Brain Three – The emotional brain

Brain three, the limbic system, is often called the 'mammal' brain. For those with pets, it's easy to tell that the dog's excited to see you but the lizard doesn't really care (a reptile only has brains one and two). Brain three is also called the socio-emotional part of the brain, as it's primarily concerned with feelings and emotional responses rather than logic or facts. This is where a child learns to be confident, resilient, creative and social – all attributes they will later need to maximise the potential of brain four.

Brain Four – Advanced functioning

While emotions *come from* brain three, our *ability to control them* is located in brain four, the frontal cortex. This brain begins to consciously control emotions from age three, but in short bursts and usually with significant help from a calming, encouraging adult. From about age seven until somewhere on average in the 20s, brain four takes centre stage. It has a break in the middle, called *adolescence*, where it essentially shuts for renovations for around three years. Brain four partially exists in other mammals but it's essentially what distinguishes us as humans (and we have a lot more of brain four than any other creature). Brain four contains our executive functions such as self-control, advanced empathy, control of emotions, advanced cognition, our conscious virtues and higher intelligence. As such, this brain is the one most aligned with positive life outcomes, by nearly every measure of success.

When all four brains are matured and wired up, we're adults! While an average age of mid-20s is often referenced, the age can range from 18 years for a first-born female to 32 years for a male that is not first-born – quite a different range to what popular culture wants us to believe. Furthermore, not all adults are equal in terms of brain development (particularly brain four). To reach its full potential – and forgive us for being a bit repetitive – brain four's development depends on what's underneath and the needs of brains one, two and three being met.

DEVELOPING THE BRAIN

Congratulations, you've graduated Neuroscience 101! If you didn't know before, you now understand the brain has four parts; they develop in turn; and the quality of development depends on prior development. With this in mind, the following is a guide to what the brain needs at different stages of life.

Birth–12 months – indulgence and partnership

Here we're talking brain one and survival. This phase is challenging, as every parent knows, but in terms of brain development it is also straightforward. In this period, the brain needs to establish safety and trust, which mainly depends on the quality of partnership with the primary caregiver. In general terms, the more responsive a caregiver, the better (or at least more likely) the outcomes for children later in life. In this phase, we can follow human instinct and spoil children because, from a neurological point of view, it's pretty much impossible to over-indulge a baby with safety and trust.

6–18 months – autonomy and freedom of movement

This phase, focused on building brain two, takes many people by surprise. In referring to *autonomy*, this relates to letting a baby feed its own motor-skill development (use of muscles) and largely keeping out of their way! Providing an environment that encourages exploration is obviously a good thing, but this is mostly about safety and encouragement (and not baby-traps like bouncers). If we take charge, such as propping up a child on a pillow, how will a child learn to use their muscles to sit up? Even when it comes to 'teaching' a child to walk – what feels like a parenting right-of-passage – a child's ability to walk is already encoded in their genes, in the same way genes drive the blooming of a rose. You won't accelerate its bloom by peeling back a rose's petals; what's required is the ideal environment for the blooming process to naturally unfold.

18 months to 7 years – self-belief and a love of learning

This phase is a blended recipe for brains two and three, particularly related to the formation and demonstration of emotions. We care a lot about facts and figures later in life but, for now, the emotional brain doesn't really care. What's important is how people interact with brain three, with a focus on nurturing a love of exploration and learning and a strong sense of self-belief. It's important to emphasise that this foundation is the *process* and *aptitude* for learning, not *acquired* information (think of the difference between a child memorising words in a book from repetition compared with making up their own story). Open-ended

and child-led play, along with encouragement of imagination and creativity, are all good ways to build this foundation. And while it's tempting to pursue early literacy and numeracy (for bragging rights at coffee group), according to neuroscience, early acquisition won't really benefit a child; their time is yet to come.

7 years to adolescence – intellectual development

Where did those first few years go? It's time for brain four, which loves patterns, consistency, correct answers and the type of learning we associate with being tested, like reading, writing and arithmetic. Brain four also understands time and consequences (because these are often logical) and, as the home of empathy and higher intelligence, it also processes and calms emotions coming from brain three. Altogether, brain four is simply incredible.

Given its impressive credentials, it's easy to see the seduction of jumping straight to develop brain four. Having a child 'ahead of their age group', typically associated with facts and figures or skills forged on repetition, is a badge of parenting honour, right? No. Just as a new roof won't compensate for inadequate housing foundations, nor will great spelling from an early age ensure self-confidence, persistence, creativity or resilience. Even as adults, learning is much easier when we feel self-assured, passionate about a topic and have confidence in our ability to contribute and solve problems. And remember, it's by firstly meeting the needs of brains one through to three that we fully access the gifts of brain four.

The adolescence years – communication and guidance

It's both the best of times and the worst of times. In reality, the challenges of adolescence are mostly a product of unrealistic parental expectations, which an understanding of neuroscience can reduce. During adolescence – though when exactly varies – brain four is essentially shut for renovations for three years, leaving brain three to carry the load. Only brain three deals in feelings not logic; it's far from a full brain. It's the same brain part that, at age three, couldn't understand that two pieces of a broken biscuit were still the same amount of biscuit – and the same brain that tells a teenager to avoid school due to their brand of shoes.

These are choppy parenting waters but, by now, we have a rich repertoire of parenting skills to draw on, with the right teen-lingo and street-cred rinsed in. Above all, this phase is about maintaining rapport while still setting boundaries and providing guidance. It's about influencing not insisting. And remember that all of your wonderful advice for brain four – just what you've been waiting to share – is nothing but nagging if you haven't influenced the feeling brain first. This is where our own leadership and influencing skills really count. Given access to brain four in this phase is also limited (research suggests about 10% of engagement time), prioritising that access is critical. Even then, success will likely hinge on validating emotions first.

Young adult and beyond – support and enjoyment

All the hard work through childhood is done – phew! Well, not quite, because your children are always your children and may still need (or at least want) you to varying degrees. But now there's a massive difference: you have no authority. From here it's all about influence, which, beyond your own influencing skills, depends on rapport and the openness of the adult you've helped shape. All going well, we enjoy seeing the potential of loving, socially responsible adults take flight. And then, with the apprenticeship over, we await another critical role in life – being a grandparent! According to many grandparents, this is where we hear our own guidance and voices channelled by our children now as parents; a reminder to speak to your children with the voice you want your grandchildren to hear.

PARENTING STYLES

The way people parent – the actions and behaviours displayed while parenting – is a complex topic. There are no end of permutations and combinations that define a unique parenting style. However, to make a discussion of parenting possible, it's necessary to distill some core styles. The study of leadership does the same – everyone's leadership is unique but can be framed and guided by certain leadership styles.

The more you think about it, parenting styles and leadership styles are essentially the same thing – they both aim to get the best out of people and situations. They're both also the business of positive action (and not the classic cop-out of 'do what I say, not what I do'). In fact, if we think of ourselves as leaders – not just parents – it's entirely possible through leadership to create breakthrough moments, whether resolving a crisis with calmness or taking positive events to new heights. In a tricky or euphoric moment, think of what one of your most respected leaders might say or do. And before you start thinking of Dame Whina Cooper, Sir Apirana Ngata or the Rt. Hon. Jacinda Ardern, remember there's probably a great leader – a mum, dad or friend – just next door.

When it comes to parenting styles, there's no shortage of frameworks, but a common one divides parenting into four styles: *Authoritative, Authoritarian, Permissive* and *Uninvolved*.[3] They're hardly the most engaging labels so, while respecting the research, we'll give you another take. First, though, to avoid putting yourself in a box – which we're *not* suggesting – it's important to emphasise that every parent probably uses *all* four styles amongst the challenges of daily life (and parents may use different styles with different children). It's also normal, with all styles, to have both good and bad parenting moments, sometimes straight after one another!

Of course, different parents have different views on styles, reflecting a host of personal circumstances, including how we were parented ourselves. But therein lies the rub: be careful not to let your own past and biases get in the way of the parenting path ahead. For the best results for children, the research suggests that *The Loving Boss* style (which we'll come to) is where we *always* want to be. That said, it's unrealistic to think anyone can parent perfectly all the time. Context matters and, in reality, most people will use different styles faced with everyday life and parenting challenges. So let's take a look at the styles.

The Loving Boss (Authoritative)

The Loving Boss explores and negotiates boundaries but maintains some rules that are non-negotiable (or at least require careful thought before being changed). To use a simple example, negotiating with a child about their choice of birthday party is probably a good thing, but negotiating over whether a car seatbelt should be worn is not (making your future instructions less likely to be followed too). With this style, children enjoy the benefits of building and exercising their higher intelligence in conversation and negotiation, while also enjoying the security of knowing there are clear boundaries and leadership in the family.

For this style, it's also important to remember that – dare we say it – negotiation between child and parent is really good. Yes, it can feel tiring. Yes, you sometimes want to put a child 'in their place' (as belittling as that saying is). And yes, as an imperfect human you might want to get your own way (perhaps, though, selfishly if the 'solution' is just quicker or more convenient for you). These are understandable thoughts and feelings, but negotiation is a core foundation of human interaction – learning to get along. It's also a fuel of critical thinking, creativity and problem solving; not to mention a negotiated solution ensuring mutual skin in the game. But there have to be limits; the title has the word *boss* in it for a reason! We know the saying 'pick your battles'; perhaps what we really mean is 'pick your negotiations'.

Sergeant Major (Authoritarian)

This style essentially expects blind compliance: 'Do as you're told!' You might have even used those words and, depending on context, tone, frequency and volume, that could be a good or bad thing. However, the use of this style (or more realistically its overuse) is associated with negative outcomes for children (or the sacrifice of better outcomes that could have been achieved). Overuse results in children having less opportunity to practise self-control; find and set their own boundaries; engage in joint problem-solving; and (even worse) engage in the sort of social interaction central to daily life. And while a 'compliant' child may behave well with a controlling parent, what happens out of sight with lower self-worth and self-control? You get the picture, and just as positive situations spiral up into other positive situations, negative situations can spiral down.

In brain terms, the risk with this style – and hence the desire to avoid it – is a reduced need for a child to use brain four. It can also lead to a more aroused and agitated brain one (those foundations of security and trust) from a child staying on high alert for the *Sergeant Major*. If you do associate with this style, even for small periods of time, have a good think about whether outcomes can be achieved another way (this book has some ideas).

Parent as Friend (Permissive)

This style is associated with letting a child lead with minimal or no attention to boundaries (or less boundaries than would be optimal). A parent characterised by this style typically wants to be liked; an understandable desire but one that risks wanting to always please a child. While the style, used appropriately, can be an important part of the parent–child attachment process and can give children a sense of standing, autonomy and confidence, overuse will fail to set sufficient boundaries for children to feel secure, guided and led.

Boundaries are restrictions, and pursuing freedom is a normal part of growing up (and even being human). But feeling secure and led by boundaries (great for brain one) also gives a sense of freedom, and avoids having to worry about what the boundary should be or the fear of the unknown. To use adult examples, think of how reassuring it is that other people stop at a red traffic light, or even what a relief it is when your partner has already sorted dinner after a busy day. In both cases, you just don't need to worry. So it's the overuse (too permissive) that could cause concerns.

Hands-off Parent (Uninvolved)

The academic title for this style, Uninvolved, pretty much says it all. If we start at this style's extreme, it's neglect. This is the worst type of harm to brain development because it gives the brain nothing to respond to, and nothing to grow in response to. (While physical abuse causes the brain to develop in ways associated with aggression and risky behaviours, the brain is still growing.)

Having said that, if you think of happy childhood memories, chances are at least some involved adventure and limited if any presence of a parent or authority figure. Furthermore, for many people, some of those memories might include the breaking of a rule, associated with feelings of creativity or innovation; or a euphoric moment associated with risk-taking on an off-limits flying fox. So some parental 'uninvolvement' (a new word!) facilitates happy childhoods. If we turn this on its head, a parent who is overinvolved gives less room for independent child-led development, risking slower brain development: 'My parent seems to always know better and thinks I can't work anything out, so maybe I'm far less capable than I think.' From there, it's not a big journey to problems with self-esteem, less experimentation, lower initiative, and so on. Again, strike the right balance – enjoy being both involved and uninvolved.

A comment on style mix

So how do you feel about your style(s)? What's your home-base style? Do you recognise some or all styles in your parenting? As you reflect, we have to remind you of what the research suggests: any move away from *The Loving Boss* risks children's outcomes being lower than they otherwise could be. These are real-world studied results, not assertions.[4] As such, we encourage all parents to keep striving to be *The Loving Boss* while minimising other styles. This may sound counter-intuitive at first: 'What are these guys saying – I have to assertively control my child on occasions.' Well, not quite. What you have to do is be firm and even assertive with your child, like in the seatbelt example, *delivered in a caring and loving way*. If we're honest with ourselves, it's possible to be constructively open *all of the time*, including being directive where appropriate. We know we don't always achieve this but, when it comes to child wellbeing, why give up the aim?

The acceptance of both parenting imperfection and the aspirational aim leads to a really important point – just keep moving in the right direction! (And we're moving to 'being your best' just below.) There's a big difference between being, for example, the *Sergeant Major* a lot of the time versus once in a blue moon. Or, for another massive contrast, between hitting children (which we, like the law, don't condone) versus yelling angrily 'go to your room'. So, it can be hard to completely avoid using less desirable styles, but use them less and reduce their impact. It's a funny way to put it, but if you can't completely stop being a *Sergeant Major*, be a much gentler version less often.

It's also natural to wonder about changes in parenting style as children grow. On that, there's not a whole lot to say – just keep striving to be *The Loving Boss*. What does change, though, is a loss of parental authority as children grow up, and you can't really be *The Loving Boss* if you're no longer the boss! As we indicated earlier, however, while authority naturally reduces, influence need not (or even if influence does reduce, you can still be influential). To assist this transition, perhaps think of the style as *The Loving co-Boss*, recognising the importance of sharing more and more authority as children grow. Even further ahead, perhaps the style becomes *Great Former Boss* (think of the respect you still hold for a great previous manager); a reputation and rapport that will still position you to support and influence as a parent.

BEING YOUR BEST

We now know how to parent – easy! But how do the components above get combined to pursue child wellbeing? The first step is about being your best, as that is what's required for best possible parenting results.

While we always want to aim more and more to be *The Loving Boss*, we know in our busy lives that it's the dance between styles (and trying to reduce the use of some) that determines how well we nurture our children's potential. In practice, this will also depend on each parent, each child, and the rapport in between. Many other factors are also relevant, from how we were raised ourselves (often our most pertinent experience of parenting); to the life skills and strengths and weaknesses we've acquired; to environmental factors like housing and the extent of wider support; how a partner parents (and whether or not styles reinforce or clash) and, of course, a child's personality and development path (itself a product of brain development and, if we're being honest with ourselves, how good our own nurturing of their brain has been).

With so many moving parts, focus on what you can control within yourself – the actions, signals and behaviours that define your parenting performance. (Clearly there are other controllables that impact family outcomes, like decisions to pursue education or employment, but for now we need to stick to parenting style.) Now for the hard sell! No matter what your level of parenting performance today, work on something to improve your performance tomorrow. It's normal to practise sport, study subjects of interest, go to the gym and attend training initiatives at work. But how many people are purposeful and deliberate about enhancing their parenting style? In saying this, life is busy, perspective is important, and there's no such thing as the perfect parent. (The literature literally uses the term 'Good Enough Parent' to emphasise this fact.)[5] But, with a child's wellbeing at stake, you shouldn't be complacent or hesitant about development. Even without a specific plan, by being more conscious about parenting you'll be rewarded with improved results.

Development ideas might come from different quarters, from self-reflection, partner feedback, ideas from friends and even great books! For something different – and this might surprise a few people – you could also ask your children for development suggestions for you. Children are essentially customers of parenting and deserve our best possible service and commitment. As in other contexts, some feedback and suggestions will be great (including going to the park more and playing more Lego), while others won't be possible to accept. Even in these circumstances you can discuss why, providing an ideal platform to discuss family responsibilities and roles. In thinking about development, also remember that your parenting time is a fixed resource (like a pie with four mouths to feed). If one of your parenting styles is used more, another will be used less. Regardless of the situation – a passing interaction, dinner time or a busy Saturday with birthday parties and sports – our parenting time is *exactly the same* and must be crafted the best possible way.

One of the hardest things about creating this book was leaving out ideas people kindly shared. Some related to being the best form of ourselves, such that they're very pertinent here. So, in the spirit of developing as parents, we'll share some more of the village's wisdom:

- *Work on yourself, as becoming a better parent follows becoming a better person.*
- *With the right mindset, you'll learn more from your child than they'll learn from you.*
- *Be a lifelong learner alongside your child.*
- *The virtues children observe shape their mind and, in turn, behaviour.*
- *Your sandpaper child, the one who rubs you the wrong way, is your greatest parenting teacher.*

PURSUING WELLBEING

As parents, we're all aiming to nurture children's potential, have a strong enduring relationship and do enough for our children to confidently leave the nest – all this and more. Our aim, if we're to believe the philosophers, psychologists and economists, is to build and hopefully maximise wellbeing – both for ourselves and, through our nurturing role, building the foundations for our children to do the same.

Wellbeing is both simple and complex. If someone says 'I'm worried about your wellbeing', most people would understand this as querying an overall state of affairs, taking all things into account. Going simpler, we might think of it as a human warrant-of-fitness. Going more complex – thanks Wikipedia – wellbeing refers to 'diverse and interconnected dimensions of physical, mental, and social wellbeing that extend beyond the traditional definition of health. It includes choices and activities aimed at achieving physical vitality, mental alacrity, social satisfaction, a sense of accomplishment, and personal fulfilment.'[6]

As that definition suggests, there are infinite combinations of factors that make up wellbeing for different people – so, like with parenting styles, we need a framework to guide us along the way. For our purposes, and for a tight link with research underpinning the virtues, we've used a wellbeing framework developed by Professor Seligman.[7] According to Seligman's well-tested work, we build virtues – in ourselves and in our children – and then deploy them to build different dimensions of wellbeing. In his framework, Seligman has distilled wellbeing into five core dimensions:

- **Positive emotions** – feeling good (on different levels, from pleasure to fulfillment)
- **Engagement** – being completely absorbed in activities
- **Relationships** – being authentically connected to others
- **Meaning** – living a purposeful existence and finding meaning in society
- **Achievement** – a sense of accomplishment and success

This framework is intuitive and embraces not just personal wellbeing but participation in society as well. But what does it really mean, and how do we apply it to parenting? (From here on we'll refer to the framework as PERMA, Seligman's made-up name using the first letter of each dimension.)

In sharpening our own knowledge, we discovered that the relevance of PERMA to parenting is alive and well. Lea Waters from Australia, for example, has published on the interface of positive psychology and parenting, and her book on strength-based parenting (focusing on children's strengths) is well worth a read.[8] Usefully for us, Renee Jain from a learning initiative called Go Zen has also written briefly on the question: 'How can parents help cultivate and strengthen PERMA's five key building blocks in their children?'[9] So let's unpack what PERMA really is, and how we can parent to build the six virtues that fuel the wellbeing fire.

Positive emotions

Think happiness, and then think about different levels of happiness, such as the difference between enjoying a cup of coffee, sitting on the deck admiring your gardening work, and reflecting at night on your initiative to help someone in the community. All positive emotions are good (more or less), but not all positive emotions are equal. If we think of children, they are happy when they get a new toy (for a while!) but they're really happy, of the satisfied kind, when they run free in the outdoors or finish a complex puzzle. As a parent, you can typically see the difference and often hear it as well.

Positive emotions reduce negative ones, and when children do something they find interesting, they are more likely to persevere in the face of challenge. Barbara Frederickson's work has also shown a strong connection between positive emotions and cognitive skills like creativity, problem solving and brainstorming.[10] Children are also likely to do more of activities they find stimulating, and the effects will last longer than those stemming from short-lived pleasure.

Importantly, positive psychology has also discovered that positive emotion can be self-taught and self-generated and, therefore, cultivated in ourselves and in children. Feeling good is a learnable skill. As Lea Waters has put it: 'Just as there are formulas and practices used to teach the skills of literacy and numeracy, there are formulas and practices that can be used to teach … the skills for wellbeing.'[11] In the parenting ideas ahead, there are a number that fundamentally relate to helping children build positive emotion. For example, asking your child at night (or yourself) to recall three feel-good moments during the day is a well-proven recipe for improving happiness.[12] If we include a moment that involved overcoming a challenge or learning something particularly rewarding, the happiness dividend is only likely to increase.

Engagement

This is about being engrossed in something fulfilling – usually something you love or find challenging in a good way – to the point of losing track of time. It's those moments when you ask children to come for dinner and, because their brains are totally immersed, they can't hear you … and they're not pretending. The fact that such activities stretch the limits and endurance of a child's brain is desirable, both for fulfilment and improving brain fitness ahead.

As a parent, nurturing engagement might start with spotting something a child seems deeply interested in and setting it up again. One of the ideas in this book – having a slot once a day to listen intently to your child talk about anything they want – is also intended to bring their engagement zone to you. Once you know, there are plenty of options. You can buy a book or get one from the library, or Google something interesting to share at the dinner table. When it comes to engagement – and remember parents are leaders – it's also desirable that children see parents engaged in their own challenging and stimulating pursuits. Just think of the signals such engagement gives off, from contentment filling the air to observable traits like creativity and persistence, all part of the virtues portfolio we want to model and build in children.

Relationships

As everyone knows, even quick interactions with strangers can be enjoyable, and then there's the warmth of long-running relationships with friends, colleagues, team mates, siblings and extended family – not to mention parents! Some of these relationships are intimate and deep, some shallow, some transactional and some easier or harder to make work. Some even lead to other benefits, like new friendships, job openings or wider community connections. No relationship is a one-way road to happiness but, in the whole, we greatly value the benefits and fulfilment relationships offer (and, if we don't, and this is okay, we walk away).

When it comes to children, it's important to encourage children to form friendships; to put themselves in a position where they can trust and rely on others and be trusted and reliable themselves. Amongst the benefits, children may feel more comfortable sharing certain things with peers 'who get it' (adults do much the same). Of course, parents who have a great partnership themselves, and a good circle of friends, are positive role models for relationships. Supporting each other with jobs or community work, including solving problems together, is probably better than just sharing a beer or wine, though of course there's room for both.

Relationships help build all the virtues and, simultaneously, displaying the virtues will enhance relationships. This is particularly within the territory of *self-mastery* and *compassion* – and there are great ideas ahead to build these virtues. Relationships are also founded on shared values, so the virtues of *integrity* and *belief* are also important.

Meaning

The virtues of *compassion* and *belief* – sharing love and believing in things bigger than oneself – are particularly central to this dimension of wellbeing. When we read end-of-life studies about what people close to death feel has mattered most, it's hardly surprising that they greatly value their contribution to humanity. True happiness comes from creating and having meaning in one's life; not from the pursuit of pleasure and material wealth.

Loving someone and being loved is meaningful, because such acts inspire people to live for, and take care of, people other than themselves. There's a beautifully simple idea ahead: *Teach a love of anything that lives.* Caring for family pets, or not needlessly killing insects (and perhaps talking about the wider role of bees in the ecosystem), will help teach children to be empathetic and loving. Taking children to help distribute food or presents to other people, offering assistance to homeless people (or showing humanity by talking with them), or picking up rubbish at the local park are all examples of living beyond oneself and attaching meaning to other things.

Parents who dedicate themselves to something larger than their own lives are teaching children the value of a meaningful life. What is larger? That is ultimately up to you – not just for yourself but what you want your children to observe. For many people, parenting and building ancestry will count as key contributions, as will volunteering, caring for others and meaningful employment. Cultural and spiritual connections, including religion and affiliation to iwi and cultural groups, will also play central roles – as will other associations like sports clubs and special interest groups.

Achievement

In whatever activity or context, big or small, achievement helps build self-esteem and provides a sense of accomplishment. Encouraging children to set and achieve goals, even daily routines like reading for one hour, will build happiness and wellbeing. Parents who actively do this themselves, even such as daily exercise, will tend to have children who develop similar attitudes, habits and beliefs. And have you ever noticed how good it feels to have others, including your own parents when you're an adult, comment on achievements? The more this happens, the stronger a child's self-belief, which in turn builds resilience ('that didn't work out but I'm still confident I can do this') and spurs children to keep trying and achieving. Importantly, the setting of goals and putting in necessary effort are just as important – the completed and directed effort is an achievement, something we don't perhaps sufficiently reinforce.

As is becoming familiar, achievement boosts virtues (such as stronger feelings of having *wisdom, courage* and *belief*) and the virtues – all of them – make achievement more likely and diverse. In fact, of all Seligman's wellbeing dimensions, achievement is perhaps the one where the full virtues portfolio matters most, because the scope of possible achievement is so broad. *Wisdom* in its multiple forms will open the door for children to achieve. But without *courage*, they might give up or step back when they could otherwise lead. And without *compassion* and *self-mastery*, children might 'burn off' other people, such that their achievements are less-respected or, given the power of teams, lower than what positive leadership and camaraderie could have achieved. Then there's *integrity* and *belief*. Achievements need to be lawful; ideally not waste resources that could be used for other things; hopefully feed into the greater good; and, if working with others, be secured with values people share. Achievement is a broad church!

PUTTING THINGS TOGETHER

With a knowledge of PERMA, we can all enhance the wellbeing of children by nurturing improved combinations of feeling good, living meaningfully, establishing supportive and friendly relationships, setting and achieving goals, and being fully engaged with life. And even though focused on children, our own wellbeing is almost guaranteed to improve! As you embark on this journey, also remember the difference between happiness and wellbeing. Wellbeing is not solely to do with feeling good. Wellbeing has depth. To quote Professor Seligman, you want to take your children 'through the countryside of pleasure and gratification, up into the high country of strength and virtue, and finally to the peaks of lasting fulfilment: meaning and purpose. … Learning that you can have more of these things … and glimpsing the vision of a flourishing human future is life-changing.'[13]

Explaining the book's approach

To secure this future, have we got some ideas for you! Our last job is to explain the book's approach, particularly the assemblage of images and words ahead. The choice of specific parenting ideas to present in the book was incredibly hard. We were blessed with a large number of ideas from people who openly shared something they felt was valuable and unique. Central to our selection was a need to cover the bases across all six virtues and, for each virtue, give an indication of the sub-components underneath (what we called 'traits'). For example, nurturing the virtue of *courage* requires us to nurture a number of traits (such as perseverance and leadership), which individually and collectively build the virtue. By understanding both virtues and traits, we're all invited to be more purposeful and targeted in how we parent to build children's wellbeing.

Once the traits and parenting ideas were settled, images were added in, seeking a visual and literary 'chemistry'. The linking of ideas with imagery will, we hope, invoke a head *and* heart response; something more powerful than just words or images alone and a great platform for reflection, learning and growth. The presentation of the material as a trilogy – a trait, image and parenting idea – was also influenced by the three baskets (kete) of knowledge in the Māori world: (1) *te kete aronui* – the basket that contains the knowledge of what we see (the image); (2) *te kete tuauri* – the basket containing the understanding of the physical world (the trait, being what is or isn't displayed or nurtured by a parent); and (3) *te kete tuatea* – the basket containing knowledge beyond space and time (the parenting ideas available for all to consume, today and tomorrow). A kete is also synonymous with a basket of choice. In that sense, the book presents options and invitations; a parenting menu waiting for the right occasion, time or place.

There are some aspects of this book that will invariably attract different interpretations and opinions ('that's a terrible idea!') and, accepting subjectivity, the book should be seen as a guide. Parenting and wellbeing are complex topics, defined by personal experience and beliefs, but we feel the concepts and intentions will stand strong.

Handing over to you

Let's quickly recap. We want to build six virtues and nurture them in children as best we can. We know it's the brain that does the building. To develop the brain we need to know something about it and how it develops. Once known, we can better tailor our parenting and, to do that, we need awareness of different parenting styles, and to be honest about our own style(s). We need to constantly strive to be *The Loving Boss* while minimising use of other styles. We are trying to build wellbeing, with the virtues the fuel of the wellbeing fire. We understand the dimensions of wellbeing and why each one matters and how we might build it. Altogether, we know to be purposeful in our parenting, with ongoing improvement, to achieve better results. (Come to think of it, why isn't that recipe taught to mums-and-dads-to-be?)

As parents, we are all seeking moments of parenting greatness: breakthrough moments – you know them when they occur – and the creation of wonderful parenting memories, perhaps one day replayed with grandchildren. Telling those special stories across generations (taonga tuku iho), the best of the best, also builds wellbeing. It's our sincere hope that the trove of treasure ahead, collected from people just like you, will help you secure beautiful memories that can be forever cherished.

We'll close with some words from a song because, amongst life's knowledge sources, music and the arts offer a great deal. The song's called *Nothing More* by The Alternate Routes; it's a beautiful song to listen to with children. Here we go … *To be humble, to be kind. It is the giving of the peace in your mind. To a stranger, to a friend. To give in such a way that has no end. We are Love. We are One. We are how we treat each other when the day is done. We are Peace. We are War. We are how we treat each other and nothing more. … Tell me what it is that you see. A world that's filled with endless possibilities? Heroes don't look like they used to. They look like you do.* Have a listen to the full song. We wish you all the very best for your parenting journey ahead. Ko te pae tawhiti, whāia kia tata; ko te pae tata, whakamaua kia tīna – Seek out distant horizons and cherish those you attain.

WISDOM

To wonder is the foundation
of learning. No toy will surpass
the joy of a curious mind.

Like the old fishing proverb – teach
someone to fish and you'll feed them for
a lifetime – ask children the right questions
and you'll nourish their minds forever.

Pass on things you took
a long time to learn.

Teach children to think
of tomorrow's needs today.

You can teach children almost any
life skill with the help of a game.

Creativity is a foundation
of knowledge and individuality,
so encourage creative experiences.

To foster proactive and inventive thinking, and build trust for exploration, warmly welcome your children's ideas.

Whether pots, pans or
an instrument, make music
central to life's harmony.

Encourage children to look for
the extraordinary in the ordinary.

Teach children that with
the right mindset there
are never many needs.

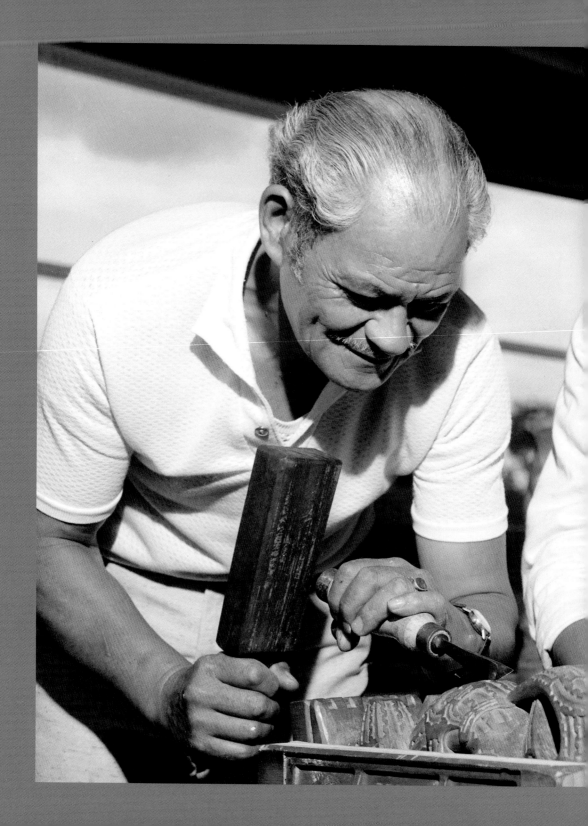

COURAGE

Your words and actions
today are your child's script
and inner voice tomorrow.

Try and embrace
mistakes, big or small, as
a fantastic fuel for learning.

Prevention isn't always
better than cure.

Don't completely clear
the way – judder bars
exist for good reason.

Take time to get lost
together; let your child give
directions or lead the way.

Whether near or far,
travel together as a
family while you can.

Exploration encourages
imagination, which
creates opportunity.

Let your children explore
and experiment at their own
pace, discovering the joy
of self-led exploration.

Encourage dreams,
tempered only by the
necessity of hard work.

Build your child's self-esteem
by asking them to recall three
feel-good moments each day.

COMPASSION

Ask your children
who they helped today.

Plan special adventures or
experiences for each child
to enrich a unique bond.

With your children, develop
a simple action to symbolise
love or a special message
from any distance.

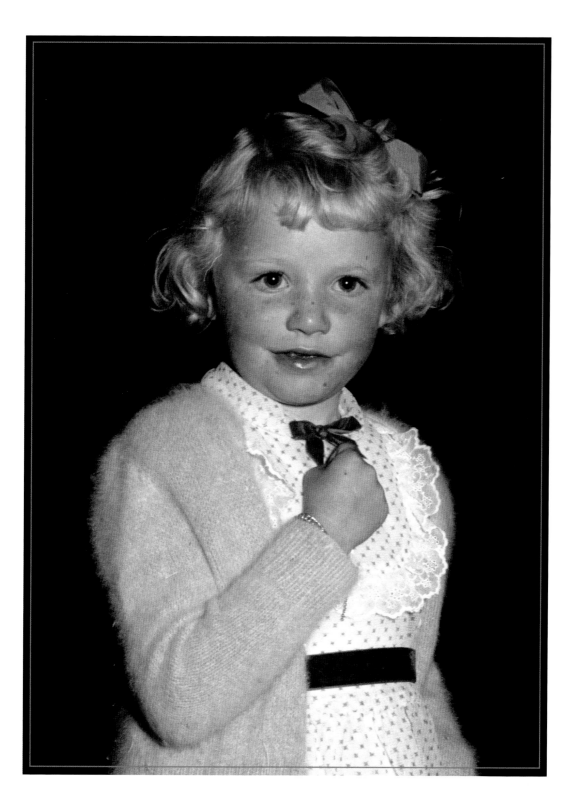

For a memorable birthday,
encourage your child to
forego some of their gifts to
support a charity instead.

Allow children to be actively
involved in family choices
from an early age, including
decisions about their future.

Actions speak louder
than words. Teach humanity
by showcasing humanity.

It's great for children
to see parents being
affectionate with each other.

Welcome your
children's friends and
have an open home.

To amplify achievements
and strengthen support,
constantly remind yourself
you were once a child.

Teach a love of
anything that lives.

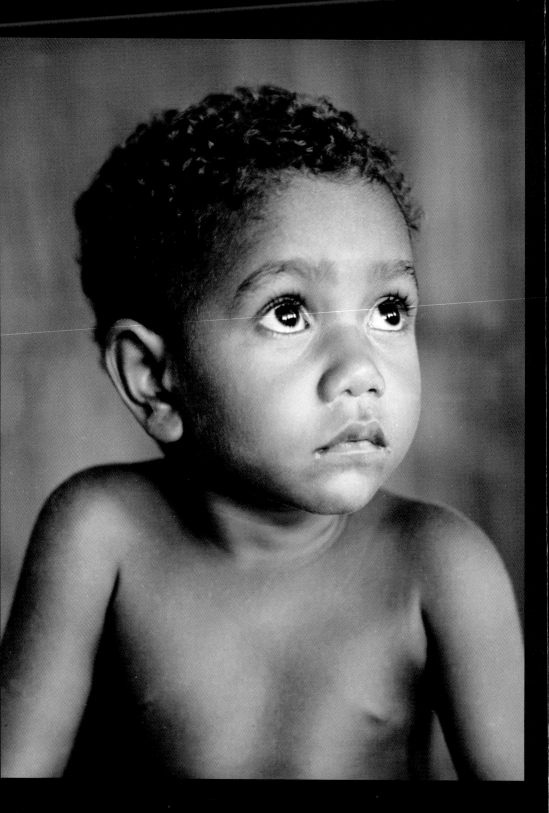

INTEGRITY

Let them be who they are.
Individuality and freedom
are gifts to behold.

Purposefully turn conventions
and stereotypes on their head.

In a world of scarce
resources, take everyday
opportunities to teach children
to ration and avoid waste.

Teach your children
that trying their best
will always be enough.

Instil old-fashioned habits,
like attendance and punctuality,
in children from an early age.

Teach children strong core values,
to live by them and do the right
thing when no one is looking.

To deepen connection, set
aside special time each day
to listen intently to your child
talk about anything they want.

When you make a
mistake, don't ever
forget to unreservedly
say you're sorry.

Team work starts in the
family. Children are never
too young to lend a hand.

Give children progressive
levels of responsibility
from a very early age.

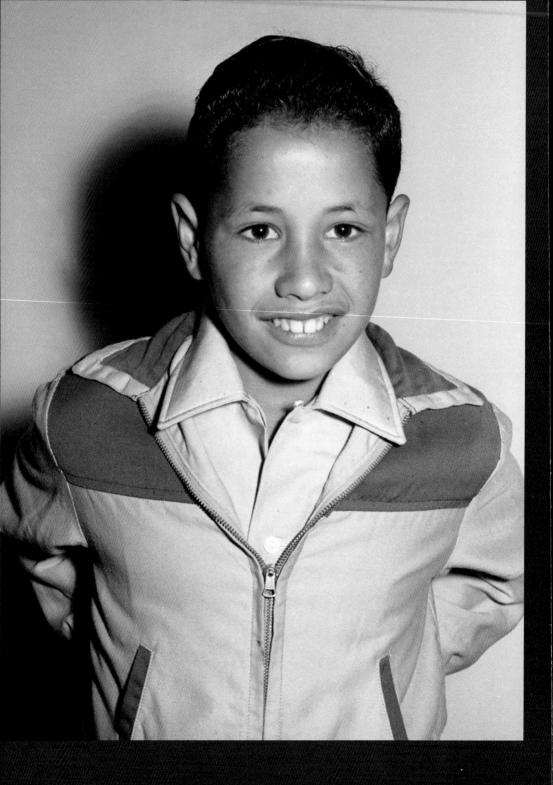

SELF-MASTERY

Each night, discuss with your
child something they did that
was kind, something courageous,
and something they learnt.

Teach children from an early
age that every strength overused
or misused can be a weakness.

Build on the golden rule – treat others as you wish to be treated – and teach the platinum rule: treat others as they *want* to be treated.

Children need to understand
their emotional footprint,
so ask them what impression
they think they're creating.

Teach that the journey is as
important as the destination.

Children are customers
of parenting so make sure
you ask for feedback.

Acknowledge feelings and
help your child name them
in order to later tame them.

When children are stretching
boundaries, remember that's what
you'll soon want them to do.

Commend even the
smallest examples of
mentoring and team play.

Teach children to look for
small gifts in the trickiest of times.
There's always a positive in a
negative if you look for it.

Dear Santa
PLease Put our
Presents under
the Christmas Tree
Love and Kisses

BELIEF

Encourage children to
use birthdays as a special
chance to share what they
admire in the person.

Embrace community
activities. It still takes a village
to raise great children.

Enjoyment is often self-limited,
so try to be equally amazed as
your children with new experiences.
Each key moment, authentically
absorbed, is in fact brand new.

What would it take to join the
All Blacks of families? Talk openly
about your future as a family and
what sort of team you want to be.

Find ways to build ancestry,
like sharing family stories
you were told. Look to the
past to help forge the future.

No matter how big or small,
enshrine special family
traditions and rituals your
children help create.

In an age of bits, bytes and tweets,
teach your children the best of the
past, like writing them a letter.

In the right moment,
think of an inspiring speaker
and give your children the most
motivational speech you can deliver.

Learn from the Māori world:
teach wehi, ihi and wana –
the wonder of life; the delight
of life; and the love of life.

Nurture in nature,
where children can just be.

ENDNOTES

PUBLISHING DETAILS

First published in 2018
Publisher – Potton & Burton, www.pottonandburton.co.nz
ISBN 978 0 947503 88 8

Concept & Project Director – Peter Alsop (www.alsopsfables.com)
Text © Peter Alsop & Nathan Wallis
Design – Peter Alsop & Anna Reed (www.mitchellstudios.co.nz)
Printed in China by Midas Printing International Ltd
Peter Alsop – palsopnz@gmail.com
Nathan Wallis – xfactoreducation@gmail.com

ACKNOWLEDGEMENTS

We acknowledge the special contributions made to this book by:

- Anna Reed, for her devotion to book design;
- Martin Seligman, for permission to use his virtues framework;
- Robbie Burton and Emma Radcliffe, for publishing support; and
- Alan Bridgland and Jude Watson, for production and editing support.

We also acknowledge the beautiful work of all photographers represented in this book (referenced further below), and appreciate the support of, and permissions from, the following institutions who provided images:

- Alexander Turnbull Library (with thanks to Ken Miller and the imaging team);
- Archives New Zealand (Trish McCormack and Terence Davidson);
- Auckland Libraries (Keith Giles and Elspeth Orwin);
- Auckland Museum (Paula Legel and Zoe Richardson); and
- Te Papa Tongarewa (David Riley).

We are also grateful to a large number of people who supported this book in various ways (including sharing of parenting knowledge and ideas): Brian and Janet Adams; David Alsop; Stefanie Backhaus; Jacqui Barnes; Jane Barnett; Jacqui Bath; Aroha Beck; Aysha Beer; Heather Bentall; Julie Bevan; Hilary Bird; Terry Bishara; Kate Bjur; Wendy Brindley-Richards; Andrea Broadhurst; Anne-Marie Brook; Juliette Broomhall; Tracey Brown; Penelope Buckman; Shelley Butler; Michelle Byrne; Ali Caldwell; Rhonda Caldwell; Lynda Carroll; Suze Case; Anayr Cayul; Bridgit Chung-Veenings; Jason Cleverly; Belinda Cooch; Jillian Cole; Jenny Coyle; Georgie Cox-Wright; Rosanna Cutri; Rachel Dawson; Shanel de Schot; Angie Dent; Kat Downs; Lance Dry; Kirsty Duncan; Athalae Elliott; Jess Ellis; Jackie Evans; Megan June Mclean Evans; Dick Frizzell; Julie Garratt; Beverley Garvey; Yvette Gilchrist; Susanna Gillies; Bridget Goodwin; Heather Graham; Lynne Handcock; Hine Harris; Giarne Harrison; Katy Hart; Lisa Harvey; Carli Hausler; Sarah Hayman; Deney Jessie Kataraina Hayward; Cindy Hawkins; Jo Hellyer; Trish Heney; Tania Herewini; Trish Heyward; Felicity Holdaway; Beth Hunter; Rochelle Hutson; Emma Jane; Sarah Joanne; Matt Johnston; Delaram Kazemi-Banks; Jan-Marie Kellow; Dympna Kennedy; Dawn Kireka; Corinne Kirkham; Anna Ladbrook; Joanna Laing; Sherideen Lange; Kathryn Langford; Ash Larsen; Lisa Lawrence; Alison Leigh; Kle Li; Kate Liddington; Adéle Lidgard; Amber Long; Louise Lum; Sally McBride; Lily McCann; Amy McConchie; Lisa McCue; Melany McCurdy; Rebecca McDonald; Myra A Mckay; Heather McQuillan; Geraldine Macgibbon; Rachel Mackay; Margaret Macpherson; Sarah Madigan; Allanya Rochelle Mahalia; Airihi Mahuika; Angela Mansell; Warren Mathieson; Lisa Miller; Min Min; Pam Mitchell; Jennie Molloy; Amy Mou; Jessica Moyle; Gay W Murray; Elen Nathan; Gina Ng; Ange Ngeru; Cat O'Brien; Jesse J O'Brien; Sam Ogier; Vanessa Oliver; Stephanie Olliver; Toni Paltridge; Amee Kathryn Parker; Marama Parore; Angi Pearce; Cole M Raen; Ryan Raras; Sandra Rasmussen; Susanne Rattray; Nicola Redwood; Janie Revell; Fran Richardson; Kylie Richardson; Erynn Riesterer; Hayley Roff; Corinne Rooney; Donna Rooney; Deborah Rose; Vicki Ruhe; Gabi Rivers; Anna Ryder; Janis Sandri; Claire Sands-Robertson; Nick Sceats; Tracey Schumacher; Leanne Seniloli; Robyn Collins Shannon; Fiona Shaw; Michelle Shaw;

Emma Sheeran; Emily Simes; Lisa Simpson; Janine Sinclair; Christine Single; Cerise Smith; Claire Southee; Eleonora Sporagna; Donna Starr; Karen Stephens; Billie Stevenson; Gary Stewart; Carolyn Sutherland; Gemma Thompson; Cherie Toatoa; Tori Tori; Cushla Tutaki; Frances van Dillen; Liz Vanderpump; Pip Walker; Hannah Wanhill; Julie Ward; Lorraine Webley; Kate Wehi; Ans Westra; Erin Whitcombe; Bernie White; Helene Wilson; and Amy Wynn.

TEXT REFERENCES

1. Alsop, P. & Kupenga, T., 2016, *Mauri Ora: Wisdom from the Māori World*, Potton & Burton, Nelson.
2. For completeness, we note that we have, for our mainstream use, amended the labels used by Seligman, without in our view changing the integrity of the framework. In publication form, Seligman defines the six virtues as: Wisdom and knowledge, Courage, Humanity, Justice, Temperance and Transcendence.
3. Maccoby, E.E. & Martin, J.A., 'Socialization in the context of the family: Parent-child interaction', in Mussen, P.H. & Hetherington, E.M., 1983, *Manual of child psychology, Vol. 4: Social development*. New York: John Wiley and Sons. pp.1–101. Research building on: Baumrind, D. (1967). 'Child care practices anteceding three patterns of preschool behavior', *Genetic Psychology Monographs*, 75(1), pp.43-88.
4. Larzelere, R., Morris, A.S., Harrist, A.W. (Eds.), 2013, *Authoritative parenting: Synthesizing nurturance and discipline for optimal child development*, American Psychological Association, Washington D.C.
5. Ramaekers, S. & Suissa, J., 2012, 'Good Enough Parenting?' (pp.73-97) in *The Claims of Parenting: Reasons, Responsibility and Society*, Springer, Netherlands.
6. https://en.wikipedia.org/wiki/Well-being
7. https://www.authentichappiness.sas.upenn.edu/learn/wellbeing
8. Waters, L., 2017, *The Strength Switch*, Scribe, Great Britain.
9. https://www.gostrengths.com/whatisperma/
10. http://theconversation.com/getting-the-happiness-formula-right-in-the-classroom-370
11. http://theconversation.com/getting-the-happiness-formula-right-in-the-classroom-370
12. Seligman, Martin, E.P., 2004, *Authentic happiness: Using the new positive psychology to realize your potential for lasting fulfillment*, Free Press, New York.
13. Seligman, Martin, E.P., 2004, *Character Strengths and Virtues: A Handbook and Classification*, Oxford University Press, New York and American Psychological Association, Washington, DC.

IMAGE CREDITS

The following abbreviations are used: Alexander Turnbull Library collection (ATL); Archives New Zealand (ANZ); (ANZ – with associated references of the National Publicity Studios (NPS)); Auckland Libraries, Sir George Grey Special Collections (AL); Auckland Museum (AM); and Te Papa Tongarewa (TP).

Given the design format of this book, most photographs have been sympathetically cropped for display. In some cases, minor image adjustments have also been made (such as to avoid border distraction). We are grateful for the permissions provided by relevant institutions who reviewed our presentation of images held in their collection.

MISCELLANEOUS

Front cover *Laurie and Kahu Morrison*, 1930, Whites Aviation, WA-03182-G, ATL (altered for cover purposes).
Back cover *Young girl and dad*, 1940s, VC Browne & Son, PB0102, www.vcbrowne.com.
Front endpaper *North Island [camping scene]*, Dec 1941, W. B. Beattie (NZ Herald), 1370-U051-12, AL.
Back endpaper *Paradise Valley trout pool, Rotorua*, 1975, G. Riethmaier (NPS), R24810387, ANZ.
Icon on back hard cover Designed by Leonard Cornwall Mitchell in 1954 for the United Nations (the winning entry in a stamp design competition related to human rights). For use in this book, the icon was extracted from an illustration on a First Day Cover and refined (with approval from the Mitchell family) to create the heart-like effect.
Dedication illustration Tourist Department advertisement designed by Leonard Cornwall Mitchell, printed in the 1928 edition of *N.Z. Artists Annual*. Minor image adjustments made, along with advertisement text removal, for display.
Dedication photo *Guide Rangi with baby*, date unknown, NPS, R21010100, ANZ.
Contents *Mr J H Hardie, Prospector, Hokitika*, 1935, W. C. Bergman, 1370-274-8, Auckland Libraries.

WELCOME

p.1 *Undentified Māori woman and children*, c.1930, Thelma Kent, F-3352-1/4, ATL.
End divider *Hawea, Fishing*, 1941, W. B. Beattie (*NZ Herald*), 1370-216A-2, AL.

THE STORY

Divider *Edith Campion with her daughter Anna*, c.1954, John Ashton, JA-578-05-F, ATL.
p.7 *Unidentified boy*, 1947, Leo White, WA-10169-G, ATL.
p.12 *School children*, Evening Post, EP/1958/1746-F, ATL.
p.13 *The order of the bath*, 1917, Leslie Adkin, B.022664, TP.
p.18 *Māori girl*, Date unknown, Tourist Department file print, C-16934, ATL.
p.19 *Female Police Constable with lost child, Gisborne*, 1971, W. Neill (NPS), R24802242, ANZ.
p.22 *A&P Show, Trentham, Hutt Valley*, 1969, John Daley, O.038893, TP.
p.25 *Boy and horse*, 1940, W. B. Beattie (*NZ Herald*), 1370-123-1, AL.
p.30 *Boy and girl on beach*, 1940, W. B. Beattie (*NZ Herald*), 1370-468-20, AL.
End divider *Boys walking down the road*, 1938, Leo White, WA-12555-G, ATL.

WISDOM

Divider *Trout fishing, Lake Gunn (Bob Speden & Alan Weaver)*, 1959, R. Fox (NPS), R24459353, ANZ.
p.35 *Portrait of a young Edgar Williams*, c.1893, Edgar Williams, 1/4-056283-G, ATL.
p.38 *Figure Studies, Farms in South [boy fishing]*, 1940, W. B. Beattie (*NZ Herald*), 1370-123-8, AL.
p.39 *Mr J H Hardie, Prospector, Hokitika*, 1935, W. C. Bergman, 1370-274-13, AL.
p.41 *Harvesting in South Canterbury*, 1941, W. B. Beattie (*NZ Herald*), 1370_U080_14, AL.
p.44 *Susan Drummond (child) and Mrs D Drummond [tennis]*, 1955, Evening Post, EP/1955/2496-F, ATL.
p.45 *Bebe de Roland, dancer, as a child in costume*, 1930, Crown Studios (Wellington), 1/2-191372-F, ATL.
p.48 *Man and girl at Kiwi Concert Party concert*, 1950, Evening Post, 114/205/03-G, ATL.
p.50 *Ratana Junior Brass Band (James Maraku, Raymond Mason & Johnson Hamohona)*, 1968, Mr Anderson (NPS), ANZ.
p.51 *Figure Studies, Farms in South [boy with dog]*, 1940, W. B. Beattie (*NZ Herald*), 1370-123-9, AL.
p.54 *Summer in Hokianga*, 1957, Eric Lee-Johnson. O.006124, TP.
End divider *John Taiapa tutoring apprentices, Māori Arts and Crafts Institute*, 1970, W, Neill (NPS), R24767819, ANZ.

COURAGE

Divider *Child in rain gear riding a pony*, 1947, Whites Aviation, WA-10725-G, ATL.
p.59 *Birthday boy*, 1959, Rykenberg Photography, 1269-A996-36, AL.
p.62 *Unidentified boy with fruit, Norfolk Island*, 1949, Whites Aviation, WA-23207-G, ATL.
p.63 *Child jumping off bridge at Whakarewarewa*, Date unknown, Creator unknown, 370-9291, AL.
p.65 *Māori child crying, Waikato*, 1938, Leo White, WA-12543-G, ATL.
p.68 *Lunch on roadside, blackberrying*, 1947, Robert E. Wells, 1/4-091186-F, ATL.
p.69 *Wells and Jackson families at Sandy Bay*, 1946, Robert E. Wells, 1/4-091166-F, ATL.
p.72 *School children standing by signposts at Fox Glacier*, 1948, Whites Aviation, WA-13776-F, ATL.
p.73 *Figure Studies, Farms in South [boy in dinghy]*, W. B. Beattie (*NZ Herald*), 1370-123-6, AL.
p.76 *Māori boy with a rugby ball, Waikato*, 1938, Leo White, WA-12550-G, ATL.
p.78 *Figure Studies, Farms in South [boy on shore]*, W. B. Beattie (*NZ Herald*), 1370-123-3, AL.
End divider *Group of unidentified children, Oriental Bay (Wgtn)*, 1959, Evening Post, EP/1959/4398-F, ATL.

COMPASSION

Divider *Unidentified Māori mother with a baby on her back*, 1930, Whites Aviation, WA-03183-G, ATL.
p.83 *Child Naomi Busel polishing window in butchers shop*, 1958, Evening Post, EP/1958/3853-F, ATL.
p.86 *Andrea Mercer being helped out of plane by Mr D O'Donnell*, 1947, Whites Aviation, WA-09047-F, ATL.
p.88 *21st birthday party*, 1959, Rykenberg Photography, 1269-B109-19, AL.
p.89 *Birthday Cake*, 1959 Rykenberg Photography, 1269-A995-22, AL.
p.92 *Christensen family breakfasting*, c.1940, E. P. Christensen, PAColl-3060-018, ATL.
p.93 *Constable Harry Wright with child*, 1952, NPS, NPS Album: Our Family (NPS Printroom), ANZ.

The Weekly Press

CHRISTMAS ·NUMBER·

19 27

"Take care of the
Children, and
the Country
will take care
of itself"

H.R.H. The DUKE of YORK

Life in New Zealand

CHRISTCHURCH 2/! NEW ZEALAND